HOW TO JUDGE A HOUSE

BOOKS BY A. M. WATKINS

BUILDING OR BUYING THE HIGH-QUALITY HOUSE AT
LOWEST COST

THE COMPLETE BOOK OF HOME REMODELING, IMPROVEMENT,
AND REPAIR

THE HOMEOWNER'S SURVIVAL KIT

HOW TO AVOID THE TEN BIGGEST HOME-BUYING TRAPS

How to Judge a House

BY A. M. WATKINS

HAWTHORN BOOKS, INC.
Publishers
New York

HOW TO JUDGE A HOUSE

Library of Congress Catalog Card Number: 70-169868

ISBN: 0-8015-3732-0

Designed by Ellen E. Gal

5 6 7 8 9 10

Contents

List of Illustrations

1

Choosing the Right
House for You

How Much House Can You Afford?

There is the old story about the love-struck young swain who asked the village sage, "How much money does it take to get married?"

The old man replied, "All the money you earn."

Like getting married, buying and owning a house can take all your money. But if you understand the basic ins and outs of home ownership, a house can be one of the very best financial investments you will ever make. It can also provide many years of joy and pleasure. Remember, however, that impulsively buying the wrong house or one you can ill afford will put unrelenting strain on you and your family, which can kill all of the pleasure inherent in home ownership. That's why it's so important that you understand how to shop for the best, most suitable house for your family at a price you can afford.

HOW MUCH TO SPEND FOR A HOUSE

A good rule of thumb: Your monthly total of basic housing expenses—taxes, mortgage payment, insurance—should not exceed your annual income divided by 60. A family earning $9,600 a year, therefore, can spend up to $160 a month for the basic expenses ($9,600 divided by 60).

Another rule that is frequently mentioned can actually be misleading. It says that the price of a house you buy should not exceed from two to two and a half times your annual income. If you are earning $10,000 a year, you could under this rule buy a

In a small Kansas town this handsome house is particularly livable and inviting. It has convenient access from the street in front yet reserves a quiet privacy for its occupants.

This rustic house on Cape Cod is up-to-the-minute in style and class yet fits in naturally with Colonial surroundings. Emil Hanslin, builder. (Photo by Lisanti, Inc.)

house priced from $20,000 to $25,000, but you should stick to the lower limit unless you have savings in the bank, a good job, and rising income.

The catch, however, is that the selling price of a house by itself is not indicative of total monthly housing expenses. Real estate taxes on a house can vary greatly from area to area. This can make a big difference in your total housing bill. (Construction costs also vary greatly. A house may sell for as little as $45,000 in some cities, yet the very same size and type of house could cost as much as $55,000 in an area of higher construction costs.) And, of course, fuel bills may cost you hundreds of dollars a winter in the cold North but practically nothing in the warm South. You must know the total housing expenses for a particular house in a particular place. This raises questions concerning the kind of house to buy and the vital features to look for that will keep your housing costs low.

Should You Buy a New or an Old House?

Consider the new house first. Generally, one of the strongest practical reasons for buying a new house is easier financing. Compared with buying an old house, a new house often can be bought with a relatively small amount of cash. The down payment required may be as little as 5 to 10 percent of house price, even less occasionally.

The classic Cape Cod design is illustrated by the Jabez Wilder house, built in Massachusetts about 1690. Its simplicity and clean lines are almost ageless. Note, for example, how the windows and doors line up all across the house. (Photo by Library of Congress)

Buying an old house usually requires a heftier down payment, often ranging between 20 to 33 percent of house price. Thus you might need at least $10,000 in cash to buy an old house priced at $50,000.

With a new house you also start with a clean slate. Little or no scrubbing, painting, or redecoration is necessary. And you need not expect to spend the money for repairs and modernization required by many an old house. A new house, however, is not all peaches and cream. The first year or two is, in effect, a shakedown cruise. Doors and windows will inevitably stick as they are broken in. You generally must cope with little or no grass and patiently wait for trees and landscaping to grow. You will have to buy such things as window screens and, in the North, storm doors and windows (normally not provided by the builder). You'll probably need some new furnishings and perhaps new appliances. Money should be set aside for these and other moving-in expenses in advance. Not all your available cash should be spent to buy the house.

Probably the biggest advantage of buying an old house is more space for the money—as much as 20 to 30 percent more living

A private deck and patio add enormous livability and pleasure to this house. (Photo by Chas. R. Pearson)

This spacious house offers great value because of simple rectangular lines that enclose a large area on two floors. There is also an excellent design for indoor-outdoor living pleasure. Techbuilt, Inc., builder. (Photo by All About Houses)

area than a new house at the same price. Old houses may also offer big rooms and such long-forgotten amenities as high ceilings and a kitchen pantry.

An old house is often located in an established neighborhood, and you can move right in. There are a lawn and landscaping, as well as city water and often city sewers. Taxes are likely to be stable (whereas in a new development they tend to rise to pay for community growth).

There are often excellent bargains available in old houses. Because they require new paint, modernization, and perhaps various repairs, many people pass up older houses. But even after a considerable outlay for modernization, your total cost still may be less than what you would pay for the equivalent space in a new house. Buying an old house is recommended, though, only if you like the challenge of doing over a house, and if you have cash resources to swing the overall buying and remodeling. On such a deal, incidentally, ask about financing the modernization with the same mortgage loan used to buy the house.

On the other side of the coin, be aware of the potential draw-backs of an old house. I have already noted that a higher cash down payment is normally needed. There is also the possibility of "hidden" defects due to age and obsolescence, and some per-fectly charming old houses can indeed be had at bargain prices, but they are located in run-down neighborhoods or in the path of spreading blight.

To sum up, an old house can be your answer if you need a large amount of space and many rooms. But the house should be thoroughly checked before you buy. Important things to check in an old house are mentioned later.

A GOOD COMPROMISE—THE YOUNG RESALE HOUSE

You may want to avoid the inevitable breaking-in chores asso-ciated with buying a new house and also avoid the moderniza-tion and repair work and expense necessary for many old houses. A good compromise is a young resale house, one built no more than, say, five years ago.

The house will be broken in and the lawn and landscaping es-tablished. The seller probably will have provided all such extras as screens and storm windows. At the same time, the house should be too young to require major repairs or modernization.

Design: Judging the Floor Plan

Regardless of the type of house, its age, and whether it's new or ancient, the same basic principles of good—or poor—design apply. Check the floor plan and room layout first, since they have much to do with how well the house will fit you and your family or how much, like a shoe that pinches, it will not fit.

The test of a good floor plan is its zoning and its circulation (the movement of the occupants within the house). Houses have three main zones—living, sleeping, and working. Each should be properly related to the others, the street, the sun, and the out-doors. This is one of the first things an architect tackles when he designs a house.

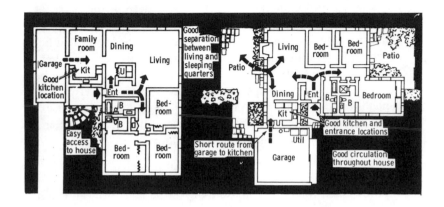

Diagrams illustrate good and bad features of typical floor plans.

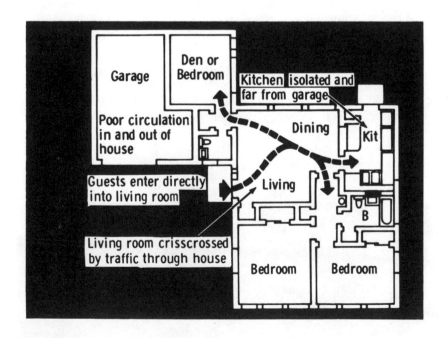

7

See if the bedrooms are clearly separated from the noise of work and play. Can you entertain guests without waking the children? A buffer zone, not just a mere partition, is needed between bedrooms and the rest of the house. This can be a hall, bathroom, or adroitly placed closets. Can unfinished laundry be left as is without being open to the view of a chance visitor? It depends on the zoning. The two-story house is an excellent example of natural zoning between the second-floor bedrooms and the kitchen and living areas on the first floor.

FIVE TESTS FOR GOOD CIRCULATION

A few main routes in a house that will be used over and over again are the key to a good floor plan.

1. Is the family entrance properly located? The main entrance for a family is usually through the kitchen. The garage should be near the kitchen for quick entry and speedy grocery unloading. The garage-to-kitchen route should be sheltered from the rain. And travel through the kitchen should not run smack through the kitchen work area.

2. Is the kitchen centrally located? This is crucial. From the kitchen a woman should have control over the entire house. She should be near the front door *and* the family entrance. She should be able to watch children playing outside and also be

A porch deck like this could make you feel like a million dollars. The soaring roof overhang makes the deck really come off well. Techbuilt, Inc., builder. (Photo by Louis Reens)

This bright, cheerful area is terrific for dining and other activities because of the large glass window-doors. Double-pane glass that is insulated cuts down heat loss and drafts in winter so you can sit nearby without discomfort. In summer the doors open for convenient access to a private patio area. Paul MacAlister, designer. (Photo by Bill Hedrich, Hedrich-Blessing)

near the dining room, living room, and patio. The kitchen should be a command post and not a foxhole. This may sound like a tall order, but it really isn't when a house is well designed.

3. Is the main entrance well planned? Guests enter here. Is there a foyer? Is there a closet near the front door? A foyer will shield people inside from casual visitors and protect you from the inrush of wind, snow, and rain. The main entrance should be close to the driveway and street.

4. Is there good room-to-room circulation? Can you go from any room to any other room without passing through a third room? From any entrance to any room without walking through a third room? The living room in particular should be free of cross traffic.

5. Is there a good indoor-outdoor relationship? Is it easy to reach the patio, terrace, or outdoor play area from the house? This normally calls for a door near the living room and kitchen to outdoors.

The usual yardstick for judging the size of a house is the number of bedrooms. But there is more to it than this. You can buy a
three-bedroom house for $40,000 or a larger house, with still
only three bedrooms, at twice that price.

The size of the rooms or, better still, the size of the overall
house is a more accurate measure of how much house you are
getting for your money. Ask for the total number of square feet
of living area or figure it yourself.

A 25- by 40-foot ranch house has 1,000 square feet. You can
determine the living area simply by measuring the exterior di-
mensions. Include all habitable rooms—that is, all rooms with
heat. Omit the garage, basement, unheated utility space, and
porch. Figure twice the first-floor area for a two-story house, and
add up the areas of each level of a split-level house or a one-and-
a-half-story Cape Cod. In general, a typical family of three to
four people requires a house with at least 1,300 to 1,400 square
feet of living area.

COST PER SQUARE FOOT OF HOUSE

New houses today generally sell, on the average, for $25 to
$30 a square foot not including the cost of the house lot. Thus a
1,000-square-foot house will cost about $25,000 to $30,000.
But these are average figures. Prices will fall to as low as $22 a
square foot in some low-cost areas, particularly in the South,
while in high-construction-cost areas new houses will run as high
as $35 or even more a square foot. The general price level in
your area can be determined from a local builder or real estate
agent. Then you will know the maximum amount of house you
can buy for the money you have to spend.

LIVING ROOM AND BEDROOMS

There are several tests for each: Is it big enough? Are there
places for furniture? Is there good internal circulation? Is it
bright, cheerful, and pleasant, with adequate light and air? The
living room should be free of cross traffic, have at least two ex-

posures, and permit furniture to face the three main focal points at once: fireplace, TV set, and outdoor view.

Bedrooms for adults should be large enough to hold a desk and chairs. A child's bedroom needs space for study and play. Windows should be large enough to let in ample light and air. It is best to avoid high ribbon windows in children's bedrooms. They are hard to see out of and hard to get out of in case of fire.

THE KITCHEN

The first thing to check is the all-important work triangle: from refrigerator to sink to cooking range. According to a famed research project at Cornell University, refrigerator-to-sink-to-range should form a triangle of between 12 and 22 feet. The ideal for most women is 16 to 17 feet—about 6½ feet from the center front of the refrigerator (or refrigerator-freezer) to center front of sink, about 5 feet from sink to center front of range, and about 5 feet from range back to the refrigerator. An efficient lay-out can be had in several shapes, such as the U or L kitchen. The work triangle is a busy place and it should not be criss-crossed by people coming in or out of the house.

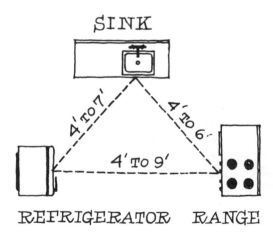

Shortest to longest distances recommended for kitchen-work triangle.

Three widespread flaws in kitchens are inadequate cabinet storage, insufficient counter length, and no counter at all next to the range. Here are minimum standards:

At least 8½ feet in length of base-cabinet storage; 11 to 13½ feet of length is ideal. This includes the cabinets under the sink and the storage portion of the range.

At least 5 to 8½ feet of wall cabinets.

At least 1½ feet of counter space on each side of the sink, on at least one side of the range, and on the open side of the refrigerator. The refrigerator door should open toward the sink.

Kitchen cabinets of wood should be made of kiln-dried, treated wood, or warping may be a problem. Steel cabinets should be made of Bonderized, cold-rolled steel. Thickness should be at least 22 gauge. Drawers should move in and out smoothly. And the shelves should be adjustable.

The ideal exposure for the kitchen and dining room is on the southeast side of a house. This will give you bright morning sunshine all year round. A kitchen facing the south gets less morning sun, especially in summer, but more afternoon sun. A kitchen on the north gets little morning sun except in summer (which may be fine if you live in the South), and it is exposed to cold winds in winter. A kitchen on the west or southwest is probably worst of all; it gets the most sun heat in the late afternoon, and this can make it insufferably hot.

What about kitchen lighting and ventilation? Is there good light over the main counter space and the sink? Good ventilation means an exhaust fan or a range hood with a built-in fan directly over the cooking range, a separate fan for a wall oven. The main kitchen exhaust fan should be located in the wall or ceiling directly over the range. Any other location will mean inefficient removal of smoke, heat, and airborne grease.

How large should the kitchen be? According to the Cornell study, the minimum kitchen work area should have at least 96 square feet (12 by 8). According to the Small Homes Council of the University of Illinois, the smallest recommended work area for a U-shaped kitchen is 8 by 10 feet. With a separate oven and dishwasher the minimum should be 112 square feet. These are minimum rules; try for more.

A large window lets in the great outdoors, and the neat, continuous countertop, from appliance to appliance, contributes to a particularly attractive kitchen. J. O. Watkins, designer.

Custom bathroom illustrates top features for convenience and easy maintenance. (Photo by Tile Council)

THE BATHROOM

The minimum-size bathroom recommended is 6 by 8 feet. Sometimes a 5 by 7 bathroom will do if it is planned well. Two people should be able to use it at once. Ideally, if there is no half bath, the master bedroom should have its own bath, located where guests can use it. This avoids conflict and obviates the hectic cleanup of the children's bath when guests are expected any minute.

LAUNDRY

The main consideration with the laundry is its location. An excellent location is adjacent to, or even in, the bathroom. This location eliminates steps in gathering soiled clothes and putting away clean clothes. It eliminates the need for clothes chutes and hampers, and it requires little additional plumbing cost. Other good laundry locations include a special laundry room, a hall, the garage, the basement, or the kitchen. Whichever location you choose, the walking distance to the bedroom-bathroom area should be short.

The total amount of space needed for a laundry depends on your equipment. The smallest space recommended with an automatic washer, drier, and ironing board is about 6 by 12 feet, but a large variety of possibilities exist. An excellent laundry planning booklet is available for 25¢ from the University of Illinois Small Homes Council, Urbana, Illinois 61801.

STORAGE

Most houses today have the usual bedroom closets, coat closet, linen closet, and cabinets for kitchen storage, but people still cry out for more storage space. Things are less cramped if there is an attic and a basement. But an attic is often hard to reach, and because of mildew you must be careful about what you store in the basement.

Without a basement, it is essential to have the "basement equivalent," a utility space above ground of 8 to 12 percent of house size, preferably near the kitchen, for storing bulky items such as screens, storm windows, trunks, and baby equipment. It can also double as a laundry area, but allow for extra space accordingly. Other storage needs include a place in the living room for books, magazines, card tables, and fireplace wood and a place in the dining room for linen, silver, and dishes.

Closets should be at least 24 inches deep and 48 inches wide, or 8 square feet, per person. A family of three or four requires at least 40 square feet of total closet space; 60 is even better. Full-width and ceiling-high closet doors are best so you can see everything inside at a glance. Look also for an inside light, adjustable shelves, and the closet floor raised about 2 inches to keep out dust.

Ceiling-high closets show how to exploit every last inch for storage space.

The chief advantage of a one-story house is that it eliminates stairs. This advantage makes the one-story house particularly good for mothers with infants and for elderly people. But many a one-story house lacks good zoning.

With a one-story house ask yourself if you can entertain in the living room without disturbing children in the bedrooms. Is there a place for parents to flee to for privacy? The use of acoustical tile in the bedroom hall, to reduce noise transmission from one end of the house to the other, is often a good idea.

Another advantage of the one-story is the aptness for indoor-outdoor living, since every room is at ground level. This feature will work out best when doorways permit direct access to the outdoor patio or terrace, and when there are few or no steps from inside to outside.

The one-and-a-half-story house is often a Cape Cod with an expansion attic. Some people feel that the second-floor rooms are sheer bonus, extra space for little extra money. But this is deceptive. The one-and-a-half-story house is often an incomplete two-story house. Its main advantage, much publicized by builders, is initial economy. You start with a small house and add second-floor rooms as you need them. But the upstairs rooms under the roof tend to be torrid in summer and hard to heat in winter. After all, this is converted attic space. So extra-thick insulation should be used upstairs and good ventilation should be provided under the roof. A two-story house is usually lower in cost and better in the long run. If you get a one-and-a-half-story house, ask about ample heating capacity for the future rooms upstairs, and request heating ducts or pipes installed up to the second floor and capped until they are needed.

The two-story house offers natural zoning between the upstairs and the downstairs, crams the most living space onto a small lot, and provides much space for comparatively little cost. The stairway location is crucial in a two-story house; poor stairway location is a common defect. The stairs often slice through the middle of the house, separating the living room and dining room like a knife. This prevents convenient use of the dining and living rooms together.

Good stairway location usually calls for stairs on the opposite side of the living room from the dining room. Or the kitchen, living room, and dining room should form a rectangle, with the stairs in the fourth corner. The stairway location also determines whether the upstairs hall will be short and efficient or long and wasteful. But remember that generous halls and stairways can add a feeling of space and grace to a house.

The split-level or multilevel house is usually at its best on hilly land, its different levels arranged to conform with the land slope. Many, however, are built on flat land, and this is often a blunder. Part of the house ends up below grade, and much of the house is stuck above grade, which calls for many steps. A poor indoor-outdoor relationship also results.

Many complaints are made about poor heating in split-level houses. The lowest level, often a play area, is cold in winter. The master bedroom, often located over an attached garage, also tends to be cold (largely because of inadequate insulation at the garage ceiling). The bedrooms on the highest level are too hot, partly because of the natural rise of warm air from below. Insist on a guaranteed heating system with a split-level house.

Outside Design and Appearance

You should look at many houses to become familiar with good design. Here are some design guides to remember:

1. A simple rectangular or L-shaped plan gives more house for the same money than a house broken up with jogs and offsets. A simple plan is cheaper to build.

2. A continuous roof line makes a house look bigger. A broken roof line, changing to a lower level for the garage, for example, may make the house look chopped up and smaller.

3. The tops and bottoms of all windows should line up, each conforming to one long horizontal line across the house. Small

windows should line up with the top or bottom half of large windows.

4. There should be a minimum of different exterior wall materials. The use of banana-split fronts embodying a mixture of brick, stone, and wood is a trick often used "to achieve variety." But after a while such gingerbread will become tiresome. The house that looks good over the years is one with a simple, coherent exterior.

5. A picture window in front of a house is senseless nine times out of ten. You have to cover it much of the time with drapes or blinds for privacy. A picture window will do far more good at the side or back, facing a private terrace, a patio, or a good view.

6. Other features to look for outside: exterior electric outlets, outside hose connections, outside gas and electric meters, short driveway with space for a car to turn around, roofed-over main entrance to protect callers from rain, and a 36-inch wide exterior basement door so that storm windows and garden tools can be carried in and out easily.

When the roof overhangs the exterior wall two to four feet, it is almost always a sign of a well-designed house. Overhangs give houses a distinctive and handsome appearance. They protect windows and walls from snow and rain. Wall paint lasts longer; rain will not pour in an open window. The earth around the house next to the foundation is shielded from the rain, which means less chance of a wet cellar. Overhangs also shade windows in summer.

Lot and Site

Poor location of a house on its lot is "probably the most costly and common mistake" made in houses, according to a top government housing agency. To understand good site planning, first consider the land around the house as divided into three zones: public, service, and private.

The public zone is the part open to public view: the front

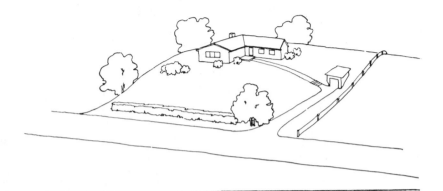

Good site design lets this low-slung ranch house spread out on a high and large lot. The garage is located at the lower level to avoid a steep driveway. The entrance and driveway are combined to cut costs and provide access to house.

An example of a poor site design is this tall two-story house stuck on top of a high lot like a sore thumb. Separate front walk and driveway increase first cost and maintenance, too, and retaining walls (more cost) are required because of the steep driveway. In all, this is an example of simple-minded, poor design that will cost extra money.

This house displays a beautifully simple design and an easy access from the front driveway to the front door. It's a cinch, for example, for a shopper returning from market to drive right up and unload groceries practically at the front doormat. Levitt and Sons, builder.

lawn. The service zone includes sidewalks, driveway, clothes-drying area, and trash-storage area. The private zone is the patio, play area, and garden. Logic calls for giving over little of your land for public and service use and a maximum for private use. Ideally, a house therefore should be set forward on its lot toward the street, with small public and service areas in front and on the side, opening up the rear of the lot for maximum private use. There will be a minimum of front lawn to be mowed, driveway and walks will be short and economical, snow shoveling will be minimized, and utility pipes and wires from the street to house will be short and economical. And when the house itself is oriented toward the rear, you can take full advantage of a larger portion of your lot for private pleasure and use.

A house should be located on a high part of the lot for good drainage. When a septic-tank system is used, it is best to put it in front of the house to facilitate the least expensive hookup to a possible street sewer later. If a water well is needed, talk to city and state water people about your ground-water conditions; talk to several well diggers and let each know you are shopping around. Avoid the need for major excavation, retaining walls, and earth-moving chores, since these can cause a major explosion in your building budget. A house should fit the natural contours of the lot. Before building, have a topographical survey and site plan made showing property lines, trees worth saving, slope contours, and such things as rock outcroppings. Before you even buy a lot, have an architect check it.

The same principles apply when you buy an existing house. How much front lawn is there to maintain? Is the driveway short and efficient? Is the patio or terrace shielded from the view of outsiders? What about natural drainage, especially if the land is hilly? This last is so important that it pays to make a special trip back on a rainy day to see if water drains away well.

ORIENTATION: WHICH WAY SHOULD YOUR HOUSE FACE?

Most houses are built facing the street; this flies in the face of logic. When a house is properly oriented in relation to the sun, your fuel bills can be reduced as much as 40 percent, your rooms will be bright and full of sunshine in winter, and the house can be 5 to 10 degrees cooler in the summer than an ordinary house would normally be.

In general, it is best to have a house face broadside to the south so it will receive the most sunshine in winter, the least in summer. The main living areas and the biggest windows generally should face south. If you live in the South, however, a southern orientation may be less desirable. You may do better if your house faces north, with patio or terrace on the north or northeast.

A few facts emphasize the importance of good orientation:

1. The south side of a house receives five times as much sun heat in winter as in summer.

2. The east and west sides, on the other hand, receive six times as much sun heat in summer as in winter.

3. Walls and windows facing north receive no solar heat in winter. Why? Because in winter the sun over the United States rises in the southeast and sets in the southwest. In summer, the

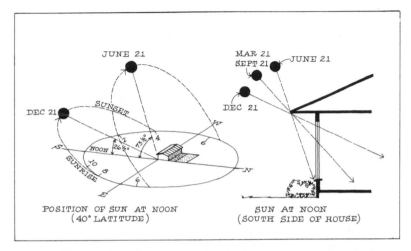

POSITION OF SUN AT NOON
(40° LATITUDE)

SUN AT NOON
(SOUTH SIDE OF HOUSE)

Diagram shows how sun travel varies from summer to winter in the northern hemisphere. As a result, south windows can be neatly shaded from the hot sun by roof overhangs (or deciduous trees) in summer when the sun is high overhead. In winter, sunshine can be had indoors only through windows on the southeast to southwest side of a house; then the low-angled sun comes in *under* the same overhangs.

sun rises in the northeast, travels in a higher arc across the sky than in winter, and sets in the northwest.

Try to have the garage on the west for sun protection or on the north for wind protection in winter. Other good ideas include wide roof overhangs to protect south windows from hot overhead sun in summer; deciduous shade trees on south, west, and east sides which provide shade in summer but lose their leaves in winter to allow sunshine through; and evergreens on the north as a wind shield in winter. Not every house, however, need face south. The principles of good orientation are what you should remember.

Suppose there is a clash between a good view and good orientation. Naturally one or the other must give; you can't have both. But a good view need not be a distant scene. A nearby flower garden or lawn can be equally satisfying.

Trees, woods, and curving streets contribute most to a pleasant neighborhood and an attractive place to live. They also increase the value of a house. (Photo by All About Houses)

The "Expandable" House

If your family is growing, you may want a house that can be expanded later at minimum expense. Does the house you will build or buy lend itself to easy expansion? Can new rooms be easily added? Is the lot large enough for a bigger house?

If you build or buy a new house, a few inexpensive provisions can be made during construction that will permit expansion later at great savings. In a one-and-a-half-story Cape Cod, for instance, heating pipes could be run up to the unfinished attic, which may be turned into finished rooms later. Discuss this and other stitch-in-time provisions with your builder. These may save you many dollars later.

When you outgrow a house, you can of course sell it and buy a larger, more suitable place. Remember, however, that the cost of selling your house and moving can run into several thousand dollars on top of the price of the new house. In addition to moving costs and inevitable redecorating and furnishing bills in a new place, there are new mortgage charges and closing costs (discussed later), not to mention the time and expense of just shopping for another house. All this expense can amount to 10 percent or more of the price of a house. If you stay put in your present house, the same money could give you a head start on expanding—even pay for a large portion of the cost of another room or two. This is a major point to consider if you are undecided about remodeling or moving.

Location and Neighborhood

A real estate agent often will say that the three most important influences on the value of a house are: 1) location, 2) location, and 3) location. He may exaggerate a little; nonetheless, the neighborhood has a great influence on the price you pay for a house, particularly for a resale house. You may see a $50,000 house in one section of town, yet another house of virtually identical size and design located in another, more desirable, neighborhood will cost you between $60,000 and $70,000. Keep this in mind when you house hunt. How much are you paying for the house itself? How much of a price premium goes for the location?

The neighborhood location is important. You will want to check on the schools, proximity to stores, shopping center, church, and so on. Look for an established neighborhood and one that is not likely to go downhill. It should be zoned strictly for residential use; you don't want to wake up some morning and see a gas station or a factory being started down the street.

The house you choose should, by and large, conform in price and size to the other houses around. Putting it another way, a $75,000 house is not a good buy in a $60,000 neighborhood. Such a house will have sharply reduced resale value.

Similarly, don't plan on spending so much money modernizing an old house that your total investment will far exceed the top value of other houses around. You are unlikely to get your money back. You will have overpriced the house for its neighborhood—that is, unless all your neighbors are engaged in improving their houses.

A $50,000 house on a $100,000 site overlooks the ocean with the surf practically underfoot. The commanding location of this house with its great setting increases its sales price—and value—more than anything else. The house really fits its site, too. Techbuilt, Inc., builder.

Conversely, beware of the large old house that may seem like an irresistible bargain, though it is really fire-sale merchandise because it is located in a deteriorating neighborhood. The house itself may be perfectly satisfactory, but the neighborhood may be impossible, especially for children.

2

The Five Major Areas of Upkeep Expenses in a House

A cheaply built house is really the most expensive one in the long run. Spend a little more money for a good-quality resale house or for good-quality low-maintenance materials and products when a house is being built or when you remodel your present house, and you save money over the years.

A few examples: maximum insulation to cut heating and cooling bills; top-quality paint that stays clean and lasts the longest before expensive repainting is required; rugged, long-lasting flooring that stays handsome with minimum upkeep; adequate wiring for all future appliances you plan to get; and good-quality windows, doors, roofing, and so on.

Of course, you pay a little more in the beginning for quality. But the extra first cost comes back to you many times over in reduced upkeep, service, and maintenance. One study shows that the use of good-quality materials and products (but not extravagantly priced luxury items) will raise the cost of a typical $50,000 house by approximately $2,500. Your monthly mortgage payments are increased by $25 to $30 a month, or from $300 to $360 a year more. But the long-term savings on sharply reduced operating and maintenance expenses, such as reduced fuel and repainting costs, will save you this much money several times over.

The following are the main areas where high-quality products can really pay off for you.

Heating

Forced-warm-air heat, used in three out of four new houses, is the most popular heat today mainly because it is lower in first cost than hot-water heat, the second runner. Some poeple, particularly in the Northeast, distrust warm air. They don't think it can heat well. This is not true. Warm air can be perfectly satisfactory in any house provided it is properly installed.

A heating system should be judged in two parts: the heating equipment and the duct or pipe system used to distribute heat to the house. A warm-air furnace should carry a ten-year guarantee. All good ones do. But it will last for twenty-five years or more. There are also lower-grade furnaces with a one-year guarantee made chiefly for the development market, where low cost is more important.

The air blower inside the furnace should be belt-driven with a pulley much like an automobile's fan belt. Cheap furnaces usually have what is called a direct-drive blower; it is directly connected to the same shaft as its electric motor. The blower forcefully circulates the warm air from the furnace to the house.

These key characteristics—ten-year guarantee and belt-driven blower mechanism—are two of the principal differences between a good furnace and the cheap kind. The good furnace can be guaranteed for ten years because it has a thicker, better-made heating chamber. Many manufacturers offer both kinds, so you cannot go by brand name alone. Although the total cost of a heating system may run about $850 to $1,500 for a house, a good-quality furnace will usually cost only about 5 percent, or $50 to $75, more than the cheapest furnace.

The design and installation of the air-duct system are crucial. A poor duct job is the chief reason why many warm-air heating systems do not heat well. The recommended duct design is called perimeter duct distribution. The warm-air discharge outlets are located around the exterior walls of your house (the house perimeter), mostly under windows. Warm air from the furnace is discharged into each room at the source of the greatest cold. This is the key to good heating. In general, you should see at least one warm-air outlet register for every exposed wall. With warm-air heat, insist that the system be adjusted for continuous air circulation, and that the air filter be easily removable for cleaning.

The first question to ask about hot-water, steam, and radiant heat concerns the heating boiler. Is it a cast-iron or a steel boiler? Cast-iron boilers are normally guaranteed for twenty to twenty-five years and are recommended if you have hard water. Steel boilers are more susceptible to corrosion from hard water and are usually guaranteed for only a year. They are not recommended if you have very hard water unless you also have a water softener.

A cast-iron boiler should carry the seal of the Institute of Boiler & Radiator Manufacturers (IBR). A steel boiler should carry the Steel Boiler Institute (SBI) stamp. Both kinds should carry the H seal of the American Society of Mechanical Engineers (ASME).

The best radiators today are usually baseboard ones, which are long, low, spread-out radiators about 7 to 9 inches high. There are two main kinds: the cast-iron and the nonferrous, which have aluminum or copper fins. Like boilers, cast-iron baseboard radiators cost a little more but last longer. A frequent complaint about the aluminum and copper baseboards is that they can be noisy. Regardless of type, every baseboard radiator should conform to the standards of the IBR.

A radiant hot-water heating system will use the same heating boiler as a regular hot-water or steam system. The house is heated by pipes imbedded in the floor, usually a concrete floor, through which heated water flows from the boiler. Radiant heat had a short spell of great popularity in the early 1950's but is less popular today. It can provide very comfortable warmth underfoot. But if a pipe leak occurs, the concrete floor has to be dug up.

Which fuel: gas or oil? You can choose either regardless of whether you have warm-air or hot-water heat. In general, gas has the edge over oil heat, provided you have low-cost natural gas. By and large, gas tends to give cleaner heat, is lower in first cost, and requires less service, and gas burners last longer than oil burners. But beware of gas if your local gas rates are steep, for then your fuel bills may climb painfully high.

If natural gas is available locally, gas will generally, but not always, be cheaper. Oil costs today average about 50¢ a gallon, more or less. Gas heat is generally competitive with 50¢ oil when gas costs run about 42¢ per therm. The therm is a standard measuring unit for gas. Call your gas company to find out what your cost per therm is. If in doubt about the comparative cost of oil and gas, talk to the gas company people and to oil dealers.

Electric heat is economical only where electric rates are low. Operating costs are competitive with oil or gas only when the electric rate is no more than 1.5¢ to 2.5¢ per kilowatt hour. If in doubt, don't be talked into electric heat before you've checked with your electric company officials.

On the other hand, electric heat can be great and also be your best bet for heating even if you pay a *little* more for it each winter than you would for gas or oil heat. This, however, is chiefly when you get it in a new house. Then a chimney is not needed (one is needed with gas or oil heat), which reduces the house construction cost. You can have an all-electric house, which means no need—and expense—for a gas line to the house. Service and repair bills are usually lower each year with electric heat, since there is no big furnace or temperamental burner mechanism to be coddled, adjusted, and repaired off and on. But remember that to keep down heating bills, electric heat requires—nay, *demands*—that a house be much more heavily insulated than for gas or oil heat (though the extra insulation cost is not as much as you may think), and in a cold climate insulated glass or storm windows and doors are also virtually mandatory.

Before choosing electric heat, get the full facts on it from your electric company, and remember to ask for an estimate from them, in writing, of the annual cost for heating your house by electricity.

Insulation

Recent research shows that most houses today are underinsulated. Many a new house has only the ceilings and not the walls insulated. This is unforgivable penny-pinching in a cold climate. A recent study shows that when a typical 1,200-square-foot house is really well insulated, total heating and cooling bills can be reduced to an average of $150 a year, or less than $13 a month nearly anywhere in the continental United States. Don't skimp on insulation!

Houses in the North should get from 2 to 3 inches of bulk insulation in their walls; at least 3 inches in the ceiling if you have an attic and at least 6 inches if you have a flat or shed roof with no

Blankets of extra-thick insulation within the walls and ceiling are the number-one way to keep down winter fuel bills. They also help keep a house cool in summer. (Photo by All About Houses)

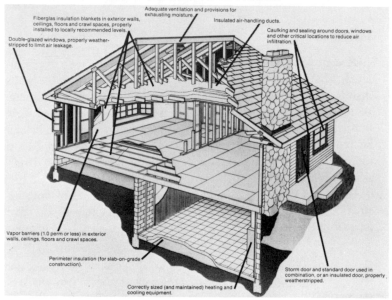

Recipe for a low-cost energy house. (Owens-Corning Fiberglass Corporation)

attic and in air-conditioned houses; or the equivalent in aluminum-foil insulation. A house with a concrete ground floor requires 2 to 3 inches of what is called perimeter insulation around the entire outer edge of the concrete. This should be an inorganic board insulation such as mineral wool.

If a house has a crawl space, the floor should be protected by at least 3 inches of insulation directly underneath, or around the inside of the foundation walls if the crawl space is heated. Insulation should be used for all walls next to an unheated space such as the garage, the floors of rooms above the garage, around dormers, and under any raised part of the house whose floor is exposed to outdoor cold. Regardless of location, houses with air conditioning or electric heat should conform to the 10–3½–3 formula: at least 10 inches under the roof, 3½ for walls, and 3 for floors.

In general, the kind of insulation most recommended is mineral wool, which is bug-proof and fire-resistant. Included in this category are rock wool and glass fiber (fiber glass). There are also wood fiber, cotton, and macerated paper. These require chemical treatment to make them resistant to fire and bugs.

Regardless of the kind of insulation, make sure it comes with a vapor barrier. This is very important. Vapor barriers prevent vapor infiltration of the internal structure of a house and help prevent moisture trouble such as peeling paint and wood rot. A vapor barrier is a layer of vapor-impermeable paper or foil or a polyethylene sheet on one side of the insulation. Vapor bar-

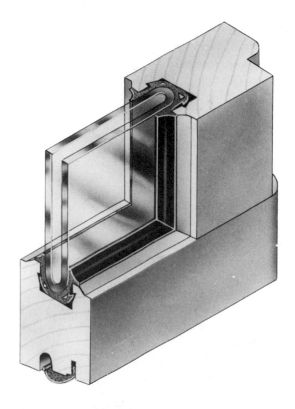

Double-glass windows cut heat loss from a house by 50 percent, compared with single-pane windows.

riers should be mandatory for almost all houses, except perhaps in a very warm climate.

A well-insulated house also calls for weather stripping around all doors and windows. According to University of Minnesota tests, weather stripping can reduce heat loss as much as 37 percent.

Wiring

According to a leading building magazine, "In many large projects half the homebuyers have to spend nearly $150 within six months for additional electric service that the builder could have provided during construction for less than $30." When wiring is put in properly, not only will you save money, but there will be little danger from overloaded circuits. There are three parts of the wiring to check:

1. Electric capacity: The minimum capacity recommended for most houses today is a three-wire, 220-volt, 100-ampere service. A larger 150- to 200-ampere service may be needed if you have an electric range, electric heat, or a house of more than 3,000 square feet. The capacity is usually marked on the main electric board. The term "three-wire" means you sometimes can actually see three separate wires running overhead from the street to the house, not just two. Otherwise the three wires might be in one cable or underground.

2. The number of branch electric circuits (wires) from the main switch box to the house: Most houses need at least ten or twelve separate circuits but get only four or five. If you have much electrical equipment, many appliances, or a large house, you may need at least fifteen to twenty circuits. Each individual circuit is represented by a separate fuse or a circuit breaker. It also pays to have two or three spare circuits for a future air-conditioner, drier, or workshop.

3. Ample electric outlets and switches: The rule for outlets is one for every 12 feet of wall, since lamps and appliances have 6-foot cords, and closer than 12 feet when a door comes between two. The kitchen should have a series of outlets above the

countertop to handle appliances safely. There should be light switches at the entrance to every room, at the top and bottom of stairs, and at garage and basement doors.

Electrical display illustrates the arterial wiring system of a house.

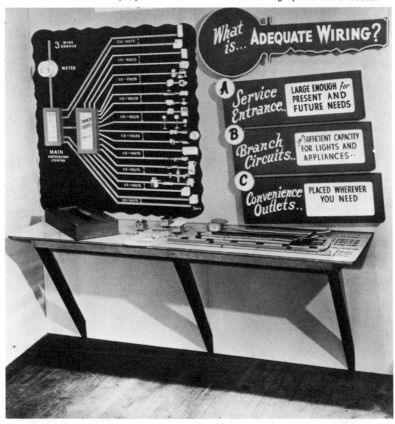

Termites and Decay

Built-in protection against termites is recommended for nearly all houses everywhere, particularly in the Southeast, the Gulf States, the Mississippi and Ohio valleys, the Atlantic seaboard, and southern California.

There are five methods of termite protection: soil poisoning, chemically treated wood, metal shields, reinforced-concrete

Termites burrow up and into a house through deceptive, mud-encased termite tunnels, sometimes seen only as "dirt" streaks on walls. Sometimes they're inside the walls and beams and then even more difficult to discover. (Photo by All About Houses)

foundation walls, and reinforced-concrete foundation caps. Ask for one or more of these, and at least the first or the second. Soil poisoning of the ground around the house consists of a chemical spray which will keep termites away for five to ten years; then it should be done again. Treated wood gives excellent permanent protection, but the expense limits it to the main wood base of the house. Neither shields nor concrete foundations nor caps are considered adequate by themselves; other protection is also needed.

In addition, all wooden parts of the house should be at least 8 inches above the ground. Dead tree stumps should be pulled pulled out and removed, since they attract termites. No wood of any kind should be kept within 20 feet of a house. Finally and perhaps most important is an annual termite inspection done by an expert. Protecting a house against termites also helps to prevent wood decay (wood rot), another major cause of structural damage. Dry wood does not decay. So keep all parts of the house dry and well ventilated. This puts added emphasis on having attic and crawl-space ventilators.

The Water Heater

This is one of the first major parts to fail in houses. Many go bad in three or four years. The causes are low-quality and undersized units that are pressed beyond their capacity.

A glass-lined hot-water heater is the most popular, and it should be a high efficiency model for low energy use. Ask about the guarantee. The best ones are guaranteed for ten to fifteen years. Others are guaranteed for only a year. Check the exact guarantee wording, since some so-called five- or even ten- and fifteen-year guarantees promise a new unit free only if the unit fails within a year; after that you get partial credit toward a new unit on a sliding scale according to how long you've had the heater. A good hot-water heater guaranteed for ten or fifteen years costs about $35 or $40 more than a cheap unit.

The cheapest hot-water heaters come with galvanized iron tanks and are seldom guaranteed for more than a year. This kind of unit, however, may be a bargain in areas with hard water, such as parts of the Midwest and California. Lime in the water forms a protective film inside the tank and prevents corrosion. But a galvanized tank is a poor buy in other places, particularly in areas with soft water. Soft water is fine for washing hair, but the high oxygen content of soft water is murder for an ordinary hot-water heater. You should have a good glass unit or an aluminum-ceramic one or, best of all, a copper heater.

Gas hot-water heaters for houses range in size from 20 gallons of storage capacity up to about 65 gallons. The 40-gallon size gas heater is generally the smallest recommended for a typical family. The chart on this page will give you an approximate idea of the capacity needed with a gas hot-water heater. If in doubt, go to the next higher size.

What Size Gas Hot-Water Heater?

(Minimum Capacity in Gallons)

NUMBER IN FAMILY	WITH NO LAUNDERING	WITH NONAUTOMATIC WASHER	WITH AUTOMATIC WASHER
3	20	30	30–40
4	30	30–40	40–50
5	30–40	40–50	40–50
6	40–50	40–50	50–65
7	40–50	50–65	65

An electric hot-water heater must be larger than a gas one for the same house. A minimum of 66 gallons' capacity is needed by most families. An 80-gallon tank is recommended if you have an automatic clothes washer. In general, gas provides hot water faster and cheaper than electricity.

Ask about the recovery rate of the heater, regardless of its type and size. This indicates how fast the heater can bounce back and heat new hot water when you need a lot at once. The recovery rate should be at least 30 gallons of hot water an hour, heated over a range of 100 degrees.

If you get an indirect hot-water heater (which is integral with the hot-water-heating boiler), you should insist that it have an IWH rating. This means Indirect Water Heater and is a quality safeguard. The capacity of an indirect hot-water heater should be at least 2.75 gallons per minute for a one-bath home, 3.5 gpm with two baths, and 4 gpm for more than two baths or if you have a large family.

3

Judging the Structure of a House

Much special knowledge and experience are needed to judge and evaluate the structure of a house. By and large, you must depend on the integrity and ability of the builder and architect.

When you build you can request that the plans conform to the construction rules of the Federal Housing Administration. This can be part of your contract even if you do not get an FHA-insured mortgage. A copy of the FHA's Minimum Property Standards can be had for $2.00 from the Government Printing Office, Washington, D.C. 20402. It is an excellent reference guide.

The prevention of structural damage due to water and moisture requires special attention. These are the biggest single causes of deterioration in American houses. They cause wood rot and decay, condensation, unsightly paint peeling, and troubles such as wet cellars. Preventing such damage calls for good waterproofing, proper drainage, vapor barriers, and good attic and crawl-space ventilation (attic and crawl-space vents should *not* be shut in winter).

Foundation and Basement Walls

The foundation should be built on solid earth. If it is placed on poorly filled or low-lying wetland, it is apt to settle. The footings underneath the foundation walls are the base on which the foundation walls rest. In general, footings should be at least 6 inches below the frost line (which means 2 to 4 feet below ground level in the North). This measurement will vary according to your building code. Footings should be at least 8 inches thick and 16 inches wide for a one- or one-and-a-half-story house, 12 inches thick and 24 inches wide for a two-story house. Larger footings are needed for unstable earth and on filled land. A rule of thumb for footings is that they be as deep as the foundation wall is thick and twice as wide. Remember that the footings are the underground base on which the foundation walls rest.

Poured concrete is best for foundation walls. It puts less stress on footings, and sometimes regular footings are not even needed. Poured solid concrete walls are usually 10 or 12 inches thick, though 8 inches is sometimes satisfactory. Poured-concrete walls give the best protection against wet basements.

Although not as strong as concrete, concrete-block and cinder-block walls can serve well. Concrete blocks are better than cinder blocks. With both kinds, however, poorly mortared joints, lack of drainage, and absence of exterior waterproofing can cause leaky walls and wet basements. The top course of all hollow-block foundation walls should be filled with cement. At least two coats of cement plaster should be applied on the exterior surface of all concrete-block and cinder-block foundation walls. What about waterproofing? In areas where wet earth and wet basements are common, water collects at the foundation footings and can cause the house to settle. This can be avoided by having drain tiles laid around the foundation walls at the footing level. Good waterproofing also calls for at least two coats of a bituminous waterproofing material troweled over the cement plaster.

The footings of houses with concrete slab floors normally should extend below the frost line, 24 to 36 inches below ground. Shallow foundations are generally acceptable in areas such as the West Coast, where frost is no problem. To have a warm and dry concrete floor usually requires that the gravel base under the slab be higher than the surrounding ground. Then water will drain away from the house. The top of the slab should be about 8 inches above the ground. Floor slabs normally should be at least 4 inches thick. Almost all require a vapor barrier material applied over the gravel before the concrete is poured. This can be a vapor-impermeable layer of polyethylene plastic or black 55-pound roll roofing material. The vapor barrier prevents ground vapor from rising up into the house.

One of the most important requirements for crawl space (a space between the first floor and the ground) is good ventilation. This calls for at least four foundation-wall ventilators, one near each corner. One square foot of net vent area is required for every 150 square feet of crawl-space area. Only two ventilators and one tenth as much vent area are needed if the crawl-space ground is covered with a vapor barrier material. The vents should not be closed in winter. The crawl space need not be vented if it is heated; the interior sides of the foundation walls should then be insulated. A crawl space should be at least 14 and preferably 18 inches high so a man can inspect it.

Floors

Cross bridging under the floors, visible at the basement ceiling, will prevent squeaky floors. This means 1- by 3-inch cross braces nailed up like X's between floor joists, or metal bridging, with no more than 8 feet between each row of bridging. Floor joists are usually 2 inches thick and from 6 to 12 inches deep, depending on type of wood, spacing between joists, and span. The first layer of wood put over the floor joists is the subfloor, which should be at least ½ to ¾ inch thick. Then comes the finished floor material.

The two principal kinds of finished flooring are the hardwoods and the resilient materials. Which to use depends largely on the room and on personal taste. Hardwood floors are used in most living rooms, dining rooms, and bedrooms. Hardwood is handsome, has a warm look and rugged wearing qualities, and is an asset for resale purposes. Oak and maple are the king and queen of the hardwoods. The top grades of each are the best-looking and most expensive. The lower grades are equally strong but lower in cost because they have appearance flaws; they can be a bargain for utility rooms, closets, attic floors, or kitchen subfloors.

Pure vinyl flooring, sometimes called solid vinyl, is considered the best all-around resilient flooring material. The most expensive, it is exceedingly tough, has a rich appearance and high resistance to oil, grease, water, and chemicals, and requires the least attention. Cork and rubber tile are usually ranked next to vinyl. Both are soft to walk on. Cork is noted for its warmth underfoot —it is a top insulator.

Vinyl-asbestos tile can be used in any room, and because of its durability and low cost it is becoming one of the most popular floor coverings. It is much superior to asphalt tile, and the step up in quality from asphalt tile to vinyl asbestos outweighs the additional cost of vinyl asbestos. Asphalt tile is found in low-price houses, particularly those with concrete floors. It is brittle and quick to show scuff marks and stains. Because of poor grease resistance it is not good in a kitchen, but it is good for a cement basement floor.

There are also ceramic tile, particularly good for bathrooms, and sheet, roll, and tile linoleum, used widely in kitchens. Inlaid linoleum is best because its color and pattern go all the way through to the base. Linoleum normally should not be used in a basement or on a concrete floor because of moisture problems common with concrete.

Walls

A permanent exterior wall material such as brick costs more than wood, but you save in the long run on painting. Other permanent wall materials include stone, stucco, asbestos, cement board, and shingles. There are also concrete-block and cinder-block walls, which are cheap in first cost but need careful installation, good insulation, and a good exterior coating to prevent cracks and water seepage. Brick, stone, and concrete, in fact, need insulation even more than wood walls.

Common exterior wall materials include wood and wood shingles. Shingles of cedar, white pine, sugar pine, western white pine, cypress, and redwood have the best painting characteristics and are least likely to warp, according to the U.S. Forests Products Laboratory. The exterior wood of a house is called siding. It should be a select grade free from knots and pitch pockets. You can tell the difference between good and poor exterior wood shingles by noticing that the good ones have regular grain with few or no defects.

Interior wall surfaces are usually made of gypsum board, often called plasterboard or dry wall, or plaster. The chief complaints about dry wall arise because a thin ⅜-inch grade is most often used, and because defects show up due to nail popping (unsightly pockmarks where the nails back out of the wall). Dry wall can be perfectly strong and stiff if a thicker ⅝- or ½-inch board is used; a double wall of two ⅜-inch sheets is even better. Nail popping will not occur when a builder uses No. 1 framing lumber properly dried out before use. Before you build or buy a new house with plasterboard walls ask the builder about nail popping.

Windows and Doors

There is a great variety available, much competition, and much price-cutting. Good windows are usually those made by a well-known company. The two principal kinds are wood- and metal-frame windows. Metal window frames get colder in winter, and moisture condensation occurs on them. But metal requires less maintenance than wood (no shrinkage, for example), and little or no painting. All windows should be checked in advance for ease of washing from inside. You should be able to remove double-hung and sliding windows from their frames. Checking the quality of aluminum windows is doubly important because of the intense competition among makers. A brand-name unit is particularly important here.

In the North, storm windows or insulating glass such as Thermopane will almost always pay off in increased winter comfort and lower fuel bills. Insulating glass has two parallel sheets of glass with a sealed air space in between. It costs more than storm windows but offers better appearance, easier cleaning, and permanent installation. If you build a house or remodel, you can save considerable expense by using stock-size Thermopane units; avoid special sizes. And take advantage of low cost nonopenable glass windows where possible.

Attic and Roof

Get strong attic floor joists if you plan to turn the attic into finished rooms. In general, floor joists should be at least 2 by 6 inches or larger. The requirements for attic construction should be obtained from an architect or building inspector.

Adequate attic or under-the-roof ventilation is important. Large vents are needed not only for summer cooling but also for ventilation to prevent condensation in winter. Attic vents should never be shut in winter, not even in the coldest parts of the North. If your attic floor is well insulated, the heat leakage from the house below will be inconsequential.

Roof flashing should be a nonferrous material such as aluminum, copper, wood, or plastic. Flashing is the covering used to seal roof joints and make them leakproof. Gutters and downspouts should be used. Omitting them to save money is false economy, since their absence increases the chance of paint peeling, decay, and damp cellars, common troubles that result from uncontrolled water runoff. Aluminum gutters are considered better than galvanized steel or wood, and the new plastic gutters, though the highest in cost, are said to excel all the others.

There are basically two kinds of roof-covering materials—the temporary kinds, which have to be renewed or replaced periodically, and the "permanent" materials, which last at least forty to fifty years and sometimes for centuries. The copper roof of Philadelphia's historic Christ Church is over two hundred years old and still in good condition.

Asphalt shingles are the most common roof material. There are three main kinds; the minimum grade weighs 235 pounds per square. (The number of shingles on 100 square feet of roof will weigh approximately that much. Roofers say 235 pounds per square.) This weight shingle will last about ten to fifteen years, more or less—closer to ten years in the South and fifteen years in the North, where there is less hot sun.

For better asphalt shingles specify 250- or 300-pound-per-square shingles, the next step up. The 250-pound asphalt-shingle roof is something of a medium grade, while the 300-pound or heavier shingle is recommended for the longest-lasting asphalt-

The "seal-down" type of shingle comes with asphalt adhesive cement, which after installation melts in the sun and sticks the shingles down. Thus there is no flapping in a heavy wind and no torn shingles and breakage when a hurricane blows.

shingle roof. A 300-pound or heavier asphalt-shingle roof should last from twenty to thirty years, sometimes more. It is the premium grade.

Wind can do damage to ordinary 235-pound asphalt shingles. So inquire about: 1) seal-down shingles—235-pound shingles with a factory-applied adhesive for keeping them stuck down despite high winds—or 2) interlocking shingles, which come with tabs and slots for hooking each shingle to the next one.

Conventional shingles can be cemented down during application by having roofing cement squirted under every tab. The

A good roof, properly installed, is obviously an important feature to protect everything underneath. The condition of the roof and the gutters of a used house can often be determined by visual inspection. (Photo by All About Houses)

250- and 300-pound shingles are less susceptible to wind damage than 235-pound shingles because they are heavier and stiffer. But if you live in a hurricane area and use one of these heavier shingles, it may be good to have their tabs cemented down during application.

If you have a low slope roof, you will often get what is called built-up roofing, alternate layers of roofing felt and asphalt covered with a top surface of gravel or white marble chips. It may last five years or twenty to twenty-five years, depending on the number of layers, or plies. Five plies are recommended; fewer mean shorter life and expensive unkeep. Ask how many plies, or if it is a ten-, fifteen-, or twenty-year roof. This is a key question.

There is also roll roofing, which comes in rolls of asphalt sheet material, cemented down and overlapped on the roof, one layer after the other up to the top of the roof. It can be used on any roof except a flat one. By and large, roll roofing can be as good as or better than the cheapest built-up roof, but it will not be as good as a four- or five-ply built-up roof. Use the heaviest roll roofing you can get.

Wood shingles cost from 50 to 100 percent more than asphalt shingles. The increase in quality over asphalt depends on the kind of wood shingle; the thicker the wood, the better the quality. The cheapest are wood shingles approximately ⅜ inch thick, which will last fifteen to twenty-five years, more or less. Then comes what are called wood shakes. These vary from ⅜ up to 1¼ inches thick. The best shakes are the heaviest and thickest ones, usually ¾ to 1¼ inches thick; they are normally good for fifty years or more.

"Permanent" roof materials include asbestos-cement shingles, tile, slate, copper, terne, and aluminum. Asbestos cement is a hard-wearing but somewhat brittle material. It is lowest in cost of all the "permanent" roof types. A tile roof should be of "hard-burned" tile. Slate, copper, and terne (tin-lead alloy) are the Cadillacs of roofing in quality and price. Aluminum offers long life, low year-to-year maintenance, and high sun heat reflectivity, which means a cool house in summer. But some of the new aluminum roofing materials are not fully tested and you should check carefully on the specific kind you like before you buy.

Special Features for Now or Later

It is axiomatic in the building field that certain features cost considerably less if installed when a house is being built, compared with the cost of installing them after the house is finished. A second or third bathroom, for example, may cost about $1,000 to $1,500 when a house is being built. The cost will jump considerably if you add it later. Insulating the walls will cost about 10¢ to 15¢ a square foot during construction, yet the same insulation installed after the walls are closed in will cost you 50¢

to 90¢ a square foot! On the other hand, the cost of finishing off a recreation room or adding a new patio is hardly any higher at a later date.

Discuss the important features you want with your builder or architect. Which can be economically provided when the house is being built? Which can be added later when you have caught your breath, financially speaking, at little or no extra cost? Nearly all builders will make such changes. But put them in writing along with the extra costs to be charged.

4

Special Checks to Make before Buying a Used House

The older the house, the more likely it is that major repairs will be required, so first find out when it was built. The big advantage of used houses is that they offer up to twice as much space for the same money as new houses. Compare the price per square foot with the going price of new houses. But add on the estimated cost of the improvement needed. What may seem a bargain at first may turn out to be a Trojan horse loaded with trouble.

The same fundamental design guides given earlier apply, of course, to used houses. Beyond that, certain parts of old houses are especially likely to be run-down. Home Inspection Consultants, Inc., a New York City firm, found that in a thousand houses over ten years old that it inspected for prospective buyers, the two main flaws were inadequate wiring (in 84 percent of the houses) and termite damage (in 58 percent). Here is a summary of important things to check in a used house:

1. *Inadequate wiring.* This is the most widespread flaw. The older the house, the poorer the wiring is likely to be unless a previous owner has rewired. Look for a three-wire, 220-volt, 100-ampere-capacity main electric board, more for large houses or if there is an electric range. New wiring will be needed if the existing board is only 30 or 60 amperes in capacity. If there are fewer than six or eight circuits (fuses), you are likely to need more. And are there enough electric outlets, particularly in the kitchen, and light switches?

New wiring will cost from about $500 to $1,000, sometimes more, for a typical old house. Figure $300 to about $500 for a new electric service and main board, plus $15 to $20 for each new outlet and light switch needed and about $25 to $50 for each special circuit for such things as a clothes drier or air-conditioner.

2. *Termite damage and wood rot.* These occur mostly in houses more than five to ten years old and are hard to detect. Hire a termite expert to check the house before you buy. Many FHA and VA offices require this important inspection before they will approve a mortgage on an old house. Ask for a check on wood decay, too.

A termite check calls for careful probing of the foundation and base wood structure of a house. A probing tool such as an ice pick is used. If a beam is eaten away inside, the pick normally will sink into it and tell you so, but not always. A telltale sign of termites is their flattened mud tunnels leading up a foundation wall into the house. But termites can be present without visible signs, so don't feel safe simply because there is no exterior evidence of their presence. On the other hand, don't give up a house and flee just because there are termites. The damage is not always extensive. The cost of repairing termite damage can range from about $250 to $5,000 or more. That is why a careful check should be made in advance.

3. *Run-down heating.* Many houses over thirty years old were built with a coal heating plant which may have since been converted to oil or gas. If the house has a hot-water or steam heating plant that is twenty-five to thirty years old or older, it may not last much longer. Look on the boiler nameplate to see if it is cast iron or steel. The cast-iron kind will usually last longer. Look inside for signs of cracking and around the exterior base for rust and general deterioration. If the heater is a large, old hot-air gravity furnace with no fan, it too is likely to expire at any time.

A heating plant in a house only ten or fifteen years old also can be troublesome. Sometimes the unit may be too small for the house. The best way to check it is to visit the house on a cold day, if possible. Have the system turned on. Set the thermostat up to 80 degrees and listen for operating noise. How long does it take for heat to reach each room after starting? A warm-air system should provide heat within ten or fifteen minutes, a hot-water or steam system within a half hour.

Also take the name and phone number of the heating dealer who services the system. This is usually noted on or near the heating unit. Ask him about the system. What kinds of repairs are needed? How long will the system last? He may or may not come clean with you, but what you learn may be worth the effort.

Installed cost of a new warm-air furnace *starts* at about $750; a new hot-water boiler from $750 to $1,500. The cost of a complete new heating system can run from $1,500 to $5,000, depending on house size.

4. *The faucet water heater.* If it is a separate hot-water heater and tank, check the nameplate for capacity and type, and judge it according to the standards given earlier. Open the little door at the base of the tank where the pilot light and burner mechanism are and look for signs of rust or leaks in here; use a flashlight. These are the first indications of trouble brewing.

An indirect domestic hot-water heater is hard to inspect for possible trouble unless you are an expert. The most common complaint about them is insufficient hot water. If possible, see if its heating capacity is given in gallons of hot water supplied per minute (gpm), and then you can rate it according to the standards already given. Installed cost of a new hot-water tank heater ranges from about $150 to $185 for a good 40- to 50-gallon gas-fired model, more for electric units.

5. *Inadequate insulation.* Most houses built before the 1940's were built without any insulation. Many houses built from World War II up to around 1955 were built with attic insulation but little or no wall insulation. Most houses built since 1955 have both wall and ceiling insulation, though not necessarily enough. Regardless of age, most houses with masonry or brick walls have no wall insulation.

Attic insulation normally can be seen at the attic floor. Ask if wall insulation has been blown into the walls. During cold weather, you can get an indication of wall insulation by holding your hand against the inside surface of an exterior wall. Then hold your hand against an interior partition. The exterior wall should not feel much colder than the inside wall. If it does, heat is leaking out; there is little or no insulation.

Average cost of insulating an existing house runs about 50¢ to 90¢ per square foot of gross exterior wall surface, plus about 20¢ to 35¢ per square foot for the attic floor. Total cost: from $1,200 to $1,800 for a typical existing house (less if it is installed during construction).

6. *Poor plumbing.* Common troubles are inadequate water pressure due to corroded pipes, and an inadequate septic-tank system. Bad plumbing is a problem mostly in houses with iron or steel pipes that are twenty-five years old or older. Copper, brass, and bronze pipes will last much longer but were not introduced until about 1940. You can tell if the pipes are iron or steel with a magnet. They will attract the magnet, but copper, brass, or bronze will not.

Test for water pressure by turning on the faucets in the kitchen, laundry, and baths. Faucets in the top-floor bathroom are the best indicators. Turn on all faucets and flush the toilet at the same time. If the water hardly comes out at all, you can expect plumbing woes.

Is there a septic tank, a cesspool, or a city sewer? If there is no public sewer, be particularly cautious even if the house is comparatively new. Overloaded septic tanks and cesspools have become a major problem in many areas. Septic-tank problems are also more likely in a house with an automatic washing machine and several children. When was the septic tank or cesspool last cleaned? Cleaning is normally needed every three or four years. Who did the cleaning? Call him and ask about the condition of the tank. Another source of information about septic-tank problems is the public-health department. They can often tell you if such problems are prevalent locally. New plumbing costs can vary greatly. Figure at least $500 to $1,500, sometimes more, but get a plumber's estimate. Septic-tank repairs can run from $250 to $1,500.

7. *Roof and gutters.* What kind of roof and how old is it? An asphalt-shingle or built-up roof on a flat or low slope will often need repairs or replacement if it is more than ten or fifteen years old. Walk around the house to inspect the roof and gutters. Look for broken or missing shingles. Note the condition of the horizontal gutters, especially if they are wood. Are the gutters clogged with leaves or clean and well maintained? The best time to check for roof leaks and bad gutters is during a heavy rain. Check inside the attic for leaks too.

The cost of patching a roof may run from $50 to $250. A new asphalt-shingle roof will cost from about $750 for a small house to about $2,000 for a house of about 2,500 square feet of roof area, more for better roofing or larger houses.

8. *Wet basement.* The usual signs are dark stains on the cellar walls and floor, and flaky cement on the walls. Look also for dry rot in the basement ceiling beams and structure and for mildew. Check the condition of the exterior foundation walls around the house. Are there cracks and signs of water penetration? Correcting a wet-basement condition is often expensive and sometimes impossible if the house was not properly built. It can cost $500 and up, depending on the house.

Other Checks for a Used House

Check the condition of the walls. Is painting required? If a new kitchen is needed, is there enough space for remodeling? Do appliances come with the house? How old are they? What about their operating condition? Will your car fit in the garage? What about the condition of driveway and sidewalks?

The estimated-cost figures given for repair work are approximations based on average costs for typical houses. When obvious repairs are necessary, mention them to the owner, who may then lower his asking price by the amount needed for repairs.

5

Central Air Conditioning

Central air conditioning is now considered necessary in houses priced as low as $20,000 in certain parts of the South. Otherwise such houses are hard to sell. Its popularity is gradually spreading to lower priced houses and northward. Air conditioning should be considered today for all new houses.

If it is not installed when you build the house, you can at least make full provision for its later installation (for about $50 to $75). Air conditioning can be much cheaper than you may think and is a marvelous thing. The provisions required include having the heating ducts designed for cooling and having adequate wiring capacity, a water drain, and space set aside for the air-conditioner.

When you get air conditioning, check on the contractor above all. He should be reliable and should be able to show you successful systems he has installed in other houses. If he can't, beware. Don't fall for the lowest bid. Pay a few dollars more for a good system. The cooling equipment should carry the certification seal of the Air Conditioning & Refrigeration Institute standards (ARI). The heating and cooling units should be matched equipment of the same brand. Ask about the amount of cooling capacity you are getting. It should keep your house at 75 degrees indoors (not 80, despite what some dealers may say) during the hottest weather. And if water is scarce or expensive, ask for an air-cooled unit, which does not need water for operation.

Central air conditioning almost always requires an outside component—the compressor, shown here. This mechanism may be noisy and therefore should be located away from an exterior patio or porch. Turn it on before you buy a house and test it for noise. A good system will not be excessively noisy. (Photo by Carrier Corporation)

6

The Federal Housing Administration

Do you get a really well built house if it is "approved" by the FHA? Not necessarily. The FHA insures mortgages made by private lenders if a house conforms to its minimum standards. These are spelled out in its Minimum Property Standards book. The key word is minimum. It will not necessarily be the strongest, best-designed house, and the equipment in it will not necessarily be of top quality. In fact, much borderline equipment will meet FHA's standards. Nevertheless, the FHA's rules are a major step forward in American housing. They are your best available safeguard.

You will do well to build or buy a house that conforms to FHA's standards. You can be sure that the structure and framework in particular—as opposed to inside utilities and equipment—are well built. But for a really good house you have to go beyond FHA's minimum requirements.

There is no such thing as an FHA-approved house. FHA will neither approve nor disapprove a house in the sense that the design and construction get a stamp of approval. FHA requires only that a house meet its minimum standards to be eligible for an FHA-insured mortgage. Some builders advertise "FHA-approved" houses to sneak across the idea that their houses are superior. This is tricky.

Special FHA Protection for Home Buyers

If you buy a new house with an FHA-insured mortgage and a serious defect occurs, the builder must make the needed repairs or he may be blacklisted by the FHA, and then he will no longer be allowed to sell houses with FHA mortgages. But don't expect the builder to correct wear-and-tear damage or damage caused by poor maintenance or homeowner neglect. He doesn't have to go that far!

If the builder is unwilling or unable to repair a serious defect, or if he has gone out of business, the FHA can now step in and pay for the necessary corrective work, whether it costs $100, $1,000, or $10,000. You get this valuable new protection for up to four years after a new house is built.

The new four-year protection against serious defects in a new house is, in fact, a revolutionary advance in safeguards for the home buyer (even though indications so far are that the FHA people are dragging their feet on enforcing it). It applies to new houses approved for FHA mortgages on or after September 2, 1964, though not to all new houses. The new house you buy must be one that "was accepted by FHA for a mortgage prior to the beginning of construction and inspected by FHA or VA [Veterans Administration] during construction." For various reasons some new houses are not okayed for FHA financing until after they have been started. The builder may not have decided to make it an FHA house until after he started construction. Buy one of these, and you don't get the four-year protection. To play safe, check with the FHA beforehand to determine if the house qualifies for the four-year protection. It also should be specified in your sales contract with the builder.

A secondhand house bought with an FHA mortgage, if it is more than four years old, is not covered by the new major-defect protection. FHA generally requires that in these cases any serious defect be corrected before it will okay a mortgage, but if a defect shows up later, neither FHA nor anybody else can help you. However, the FHA major-defects protection may cover you if your house was originally built and sold as a new FHA house after September 2, 1964, and meets the other FHA requirements noted above. It is then still covered for four years after the house was originally built.

If you buy a house with a VA or any other kind of mortgage, it's up to the builder to correct defects. The four-year protection so far is exclusive with FHA. It may, however, eventually be extended to new houses with VA mortgages, possibly by the time you read this. Keep in mind that there is no such thing as an "FHA-approved" house in the sense that FHA puts on a stamp of approval. FHA requires simply that houses with FHA-insured mortgages conform to certain minimum construction standards.

FHA's Special Advantages for Veterans and Servicemen

A veteran can obtain an FHA mortgage with a lower down payment than a nonveteran can, as low as a few hundred dollars down for a low-priced house. There are other features for veterans that are too lengthy (and too full of gobbledygook) to include here. And because the terms are continually subject to change, we suggest you write for them, together with details about regular FHA mortgages, to the Federal Housing Administration, Washington, D.C. 20410; or check with the FHA office nearest you.

FHA mortgages for servicemen are designed to enable a person in military service with at least two years of active duty to buy a house when he otherwise would be unable to do so while on active duty. The terms (down payment, etc.) are much like the regular terms for an FHA home loan, except that while on active duty a soldier saves the ½ of 1 percent insurance-premium charge added to regular FHA loans. The Defense Department pays that charge for him each month. It means a saving of a few dollars a month, depending on the mortgage. To qualify, a serviceman must furnish the FHA with a Certificate of Eligibility (Form DD802), obtained from his commanding officer.

7

Experts Who Can Check a House for You

Unfortunately, few people make a business of checking houses for potential buyers. And sometimes you have to hire two or three different experts. Real estate appraisers are the best for evaluating the *market value* of a house, but usually they are not construction experts. Getting an appraiser's report is particularly recommended before you buy a used house. You could also call in an architect or builder—provided, of course, he has no connection with the house being checked. Or call the nearest FHA or VA office for the names of people they use, especially experts for making a termite or septic-tank check.

But help is on the way. In a growing number of cities and especially large metropolitan areas like New York City, a new breed of "home-inspection consultant" has sprung up. By and large, he is an engineer in the business of inspecting houses—and often commercial and industrial structures, too—for prospective buyers. He charges about $100 to $150—more for large houses or special inspections—to probe and inspect a house for sale, new or old. Such a man will give you a detailed report on the house, tell you how good or bad the heating, foundation, and other important parts of the house are, detect termites if present (though sometimes even the most thorough Sherlock Holmes can miss a well-hidden clan of submerged termites), and, in all, give you a fairly thorough if not total structural report on a house. (You cannot expect a total 100-percent report on any house, simply because no one has X-ray eyes that will see everything inside every wall.)

To find such a consultant, look in the classified pages of the

This modern one-story ranch house in Ohio uses clerestory glass, which brightens up the interior enomously, yet the house still retains great interior privacy for its occupants (who have their own outdoor life at the rear of the house). (Photo by All About Houses)

telephone directory under "Home Inspection Services" or "Building Inspection Firms." In the New York area, for example, there are Paul Anthony, a consulting engineer in White Plains, New York (914-949-3787), and Home Inspection Consultants (212-947-8184), which also has franchised engineers associated with it in such other cities as Philadelphia, St. Louis, and Denver.

If there is no such qualified home inspection engineer near you, call the nearest FHA or VA office and ask the chief architect to recommend one. Ask whom his offices uses, at least for termite and septic-tank checks, which may be mandatory for houses submitted for government-insured mortgages, depending on geographical location. You could also try a local builder or architect who is properly recommended. Or search out a real estate appraiser who, in addition to appraising the market value of houses, is technically qualified to inspect the structure and mechanical equipment of houses. Remember, though, that many appraisers are not conversant with the intricacies of house construction. If you talk with one, you should specify that you want a full structural check, not just the usual real estate appraisal for market value only.

Using an expert is also recommended when you buy a new house. He can judge the quality of construction for you and also spot inadvertent mistakes and construction oversights that you might overlook. With his report in hand, you can request the builder to make the necessary corrections. He usually will be willing to do so before you buy the house (since he wants to make the sale), but perhaps not so willing after you buy.

"HOW"—10-Year Insurance on a New House

The best protection so far against serious defects in a new house is a ten-year insurance plan sponsored by the National Association of Home Builders (NAHB). If anything serious goes wrong, short of normal wear and tear or owner abuse or neglect, this new insurance will pay for virtually any necessary structural repairs.

It's called HOW, short for Home Owners Warranty Program, and it's available through many, though not all, local builder members of the NAHB. Ask the builder about it before you buy a house. The builder pays the insurance cost, which is $2 per thousand dollars of the house selling price. For a $60,000 house the cost of a HOW policy thus will be $120. It's worth the cost, no matter who pays it.

In addition, builders who offer HOW warranties on their houses tend to be among the best builders. Each must fulfill certain standards, is subject to spot-check inspections, and he can be dropped from the program at any time.

Insurance against defects in a used house is also offered by a growing number of home inspection consultants and real estate brokers, but again you must ask such people about it. If one says he or she doesn't have it, ask others.

8

Real Estate Brokers

Unlike renting an apartment, buying a house through a real estate broker (or agent) will not cost you money. Sometimes he can, in fact, save you money. The broker's fee is generally 5 to 7 percent of the selling price of a house, more for farm properties. But this is almost always paid by the seller, not the buyer.

A real estate broker can save you much time by showing you houses on the market. Incidentally, most brokers deal with resale houses only; only a few handle new houses. A good broker also can do the dickering on a house for you, particularly if bargaining is distasteful to you. He can help you get a mortgage and can handle a variety of the transaction details. Remember, however, that a real estate broker is not expected to be a design expert. Don't lean on one for architectural or structural expertise. Consult the appropriate construction expert for such information.

Call on the brokers who advertise the kind of house you seek. At the same time you can still shop for a house on your own. Consulting a broker about one house does not bind you to him for all houses. You are, however, obligated to deal through him for any house that he introduced you to.

Closing Costs

When you buy a house, new or old, you must pay certain bills called closing costs or settling charges. They are in addition to the house price and can run up to $500 to $1,500 or more.

Closing costs pay for the transaction of buying and obtaining a mortgage. The exact amount you pay varies from state to state. They pay for such things as title search and insurance, mortgage service charges, various transfer-of-ownership charges, and local, state, and federal taxes. You must also pay back the seller for property taxes he has paid in advance.

It's best to determine your closing costs in advance of closing day. Your mortgage lender can provide the figures.

And finally, it's also a good idea to hire a lawyer to represent you at the closing. In fact, hire him in advance. There is no set fee for this, but the cost generally will fall between $100 and $250 for the average-price house, or up to 1 percent of the house price.

9

Getting a Mortgage

Nine out of ten of us must finance the purchase of a house. We require a mortgage loan. A lender lays out the cash to buy the house. You sign a legal document binding yourself to pay him back in regular payments over a period of years. The house and property are pledged as collateral. You promise to keep the house insured, pay all property taxes, and maintain the property in reasonably good condition. If you default, the lender may take over the property. The mortgage loan represents one of the most favorable consumer loans of any kind, with the lowest overall interest rates of virtually all consumer loans.

How large a mortgage should you get? The minimum down payment, the maximum mortgage amount, the interest rate, and your monthly payment schedule depend on the house, the lender, and the particular mortgage you get. Most mortgages today run for twenty, twenty-five, or thirty years. You can pay it off in fewer than twenty years, if you wish; the shorter the mortgage term, the higher your monthly payments but the lower the total interest cost.

The chart shows monthly payments for interest and principal per $1,000 of mortgage at different rates and terms:

Mortgage term	7% interest	8% interest	9% interest
20 years	$7.76 month	$8.37 month	$9.00 month
25	7.07	7.72	8.40
30	6.66	7.34	8.05

Your payments for a particular mortgage can be computed by multiplying the amount of mortgage times the appropriate figure from above. Thus, monthly payments for a twenty-year, $25,000 mortgage at 7 percent would be 25 times $7.76 (from above table), or $194 a month. Payments for a thirty-year mortgage at 8 percent of, say, $30,000 would be $7.34 times 30, or $220.20 a month.

Mortgage interest rates vary from one part of the country to another, usually being lowest in large metropolitan areas in the East and Midwest, higher in smaller towns, rural areas, and on the West Coast. They also can vary from one year to another, fluctuating up and down like, it seems, a bobbing ball on the ocean. In recent years they have climbed up to 8 to 10 percent and then settled down to about 8½ percent, the exact rate varying according to where you live and the economics of the national money market at the time.

In addition, interest rates can vary by as much as ¼ to ½ of 1 percent, depending on the bank or savings and loan association you deal with, and also depending on such other things as the size of the down payment you make on a house; sometimes a large down payment (25 percent or more) will get you a mortgage with an interest rate reduced by ¼ to ½ of 1 percent, compared with the going rate for mortgages.

All of that means that it can pay to shop for a mortgage, which involves calling on all the banks and savings and loan associations around. Ask the mortgage manager at each one what are his current terms, interest rate, down payment required, and other such things, including estimated closing costs. That kind of shopping before buying a house could save you a pretty penny.

Also ask about the availability of government-insured FHA and, if you're a veteran, VA mortgages. Any home buyer can apply for an FHA loan, and getting one could make a big difference by allowing you to buy a house with a comparatively small cash down payment when otherwise a large down payment that you cannot pay is required. Here, too, remember that both FHA and VA loans, though insured by the federal government, are nonetheless made by private banks and other mortgage lenders; that's where you apply to get one—with one exception. The exception is a VA "direct" mortgage loan, which is made by the VA in areas where veterans are unable to obtain a regular GI

In Westport, Connecticut, this spacious New England saltbox combines authentic traditional design with thoroughly modern, up-to-date construction. Jonathan Aley, builder.

mortgage from a private mortgage lender. Information about FHA mortgage loans can be obtained by writing to the FHA, Washington, D.C. 20410; about VA loans by calling your local Veterans Administration office or writing to the Veterans Administration, Washington, D.C. 20420.

There are also "conventional" mortgages, which are the most common kind offered by most banks and other mortgage lenders. The government has nothing to do with them; each one is a private transaction made between you and the lender at an interest rate and other terms determined by competition among local banks and according to customary procedures in a particular area. In general, the interest rate on a conventional mortgage loan will run a notch or two higher than on an FHA or VA loan, and the lender making the loan usually doesn't check out the house as thoroughly as the government does for an FHA or VA loan. On the other hand, a conventional mortgage often can be obtained quicker and with less fuss and red tape than a government-insured mortgage loan.

Don't bite off more mortgage than you can chew. This is particularly important for a young family with children bound by many financial obligations and a limited income. It's tempting to choose a short-term mortgage with large monthly payments in order to pay off the mortgage as quickly as possible. It's often much better for your peace of mind to choose a loan with smaller payments, especially if the mortgage contains a "prepayment" clause.

Suppose you get a twenty-five-year mortgage with payments of, say, $165 a month, the most you can afford now. After a few years you may be able to pay more. Then you can make extra payments ahead of time whenever you choose. This reduces your overall interest; you could pay off the mortgage in twenty years or less. Your total interest will be proportionately less. In effect, the interest charge will be cut down almost as low as with a twenty-year mortgage.

A few other things about mortgages and paying off a house: The total interest you pay on your mortgage each year is a tax-deductible item on federal and state income-tax returns. Thus, for example, if you pay $600 a year in interest on your house mortgage, you will get some of that back via a reduced income tax. If you're in the 25-percent income-tax bracket, you would save 25 percent, or $150, of that mortgage interest; your net mortgage cost is $450, plus what you might save on your state income tax. Your property taxes on the house are also tax deductible. So, in all, when you figure the cost of buying and owning a house, it isn't all one big long painful expense and a major financial outlay month after month. What you spend for mortgage interest and property taxes each year could reduce your annual income tax by quite a few dollars, depending, of course, on your income-tax bracket.

Also consider a mortgage-repayment insurance policy. This is actually a form of life insurance, usually at a fairly low premium —a policy that can provide funds to pay off the mortgage if the breadwinner should die. This lets a man leave his family the home they chose, rather than a large debt. Mortgage insurance is also available in smaller amounts to see families through a limited period of readjustment. If you get a mortgage policy, arrange it through your regular life-insurance man, rather than through the bank that gives you the mortgage. If you buy it through the mortgage lender, it will usually have a little hook in the small print that calls for the policy to be paid to the mortgage lender—in other words, for the house to be paid for regardless of whether this is the best thing to do at the time. It's generally better to have the policy paid, in case of death, to the surviving spouse, not to the mortgage lender. Then a widow or widower need not pay off the house, especially if there is a better use or more urgent need for the money.

10

The Economics of Renting
versus Buying

In most instances you will end up financially ahead by buying and owning a house, compared with renting comparable living quarters. Each mortgage payment builds up your equity in the house. When you rent, of course, you have nothing to show later but a bundle of rent receipts.

You build up little equity, to be sure, during the first few years of home ownership. Much of your fixed mortgage payments goes for interest. The interest gradually falls off, though, accompanied by a proportionate increase in the portion of your payments that goes for the mortgage principal.

Buying a house will almost always be cheaper than renting if you stay in the house for at least three to four years. It does not usually pay to buy a house for less than three to four years because of the various expenses associated with buying a house—moving, for example, plus a possible 6 percent real estate agent's fee for selling your old house. These expenses, balanced against the small equity built up in a house during the first years of ownership, mean that renting is economically sounder for short periods. But after three to four years, the economics of ownership far outweigh those of renting.

A typical young married couple with little savings at the start of the husband's career may, therefore, do better financially by renting for a while. Once the family is established and has savings in the bank, owning a house will considerably increase both financial and emotional stability.

How Much Can You Spend for a House?

Naturally, it depends on your income less your essential out-
lays for all other needs. You can get an accurate idea as follows:

1. *Add up your monthly living expenses other than for
   housing:*
   Food $_____
   Clothing   _____
   Medical and dental bills   _____
   Life and health insurance   _____
   Other insurance   _____
   Automobile upkeep, insurance   _____
   Commuting to work   _____
   Entertainment and recreation   _____
   Children's school, college expenses   _____
   Installment   payments   (washer,   drier,   other
       monthly installment payments)   _____
   Church, other contributions   _____
   Summer vacation   _____
   Hobbies, books, magazines, records   _____
   Savings, investments, etc.   _____
   Special luxuries, pleasures (sports, pets, eating out,
       movies, etc.)   _____
   Personal gifts, Christmas expenses   _____
   Miscellaneous (barber, beauty shop expenses, bath-
       room supplies)   _____
   Any other expenses   _____
       Total living expenses other than for housing $_____
2. *Determine monthly income available for housing:*
   Total gross monthly income (omit a working wife's
       income unless she will continue to work) $_____
   Minus all deductions for income taxes, social se-
       curity, etc.   _____
       Net take-home pay $_____
   Subtract total monthly nonhousing expenses from
       above   _____
       Total monthly money available for housing $_____
3. *Determine money available for monthly mortgage
   payments:*
   Total monthly money available for housing from
       the above: $_____

Subtract amount needed for property taxes, insurance, and monthly heating, upkeep, and operating costs. (This figure will vary according to the house and where you live and must be estimated locally. In general, you can figure approximately $8 to $12 a month per $1,000 of house price. But remember that this is an approximation. Figure $8 for a small town up to $12 in a large town or metropolitan suburb.)

Total money left for monthly mortgage payments $_____

A few notes about the above figures. It is up to you to be honest and make them accurate. Fudging the figures will only make it harder for you later. Many families find that getting the house they want means they must cut down on other expenses. If, however, you have enough savings in the bank, a large down payment will mean lower monthly mortgage payments.

It is best if total housing expenses do not exceed 20 to 30 percent of your monthly take-home pay.

AN IMPORTANT FINAL CONSIDERATION

Before you buy a house, give free rein to your deepest feelings. Do you really like the house? Do you really want to buy it? Be honest. Face this question head on.

Is it really the house for you? Does it embody the principal features you desire in a house? What about location? Will you be able to tolerate certain inevitable drawbacks? Remember, there is no perfect house.

Can you really afford it? Face up to this question, too. Or are you truly willing to sacrifice other needs or pleasures to own a certain house?

Go a step further. Why do you want to own a house? What do you really seek in a house? Are you interested chiefly in living convenience and the most satisfactory house and location for your family's living and working needs? Or are you concerned primarily in buying a house chiefly as shelter and a good financial investment? Or you may wish to step up in the world and live in an impressive place for entertaining or other social reasons. Whatever the reason, it's your concern and of great importance to you. The big point is to determine your bedrock motivations and explore them honestly with your family.

It is amazing how uncovering your emotional reasons for wanting a house can shed light on the best solution for your family. Your real feelings are the key. Coupled with the hard-core facts of home ownership, they can give you insight toward resolving the basic questions, How do you judge a house? and How much house can you afford?

11

Checklist for Shopping for and Buying a House

Here are important things to check when you shop for a house and important facts to know before you buy one. Remember, though, that no house is perfect, and some of the best houses may be deficient here and there. On the other hand, if a house scores low on numerous checklist items, you have fair warning that it is probably a poor house.

The following checklist may include specific points that, due to space limitations, have not been explained in detail in the text of this book but which are nevertheless important. By and large, such points are self-explanatory and like other key facts about home buying, they can and should be brought up and, if necessary, questioned when you talk to a builder about his new house for sale, or the owner of a used house for sale, or your lawyer and the banker with whom you negotiate a mortgage.

How Much Is the House Really Worth?

● What is the fair market value of the house? This can be determined for you by a good real estate appraiser. How does it compare with the sales price (which may be something else again)?

● Does the house conform in price with other comparable houses in the same area?

● Is the house located in a residential neighborhood that will retain its character and value, if not increase in desirability? Or is the neighborhood likely to deteriorate in value (and pull down the value of the house)?

● Have you had the house checked by a construction expert (even if it is a new house)?

- How much money will you have to spend for repairs and improvements if you buy it?
- How much is the house worth to you—the top price you are willing to pay?
- If you must sell the house in a year or two, will you be able to get back what you paid for it or close to it? (This is a good check on whether you are paying too much.)
- How long has the house been for sale? The longer it has been on the market, the more likely it can be bought at a reduced price.
- If you buy the house directly from the owner, will you get a break on the price (since the owner does not pay a real estate broker's commission)?
- Is the house really worth the price? Answer this question quickly and objectively and it's probably the right answer. If you hem and haw, trying to think of reasons why the house may be worth the price asked, then it's probably overpriced.

Buying Expenses

- What are the total closing costs for the house? Can they be reduced? Have you compared them with closing costs at different banks?
- If you are buying a used house, can the existing title insurance be reissued to you at lower cost than a new policy?
- How much must you pay in advance for escrow real estate taxes?
- What are the annual real estate taxes for the house?
- If you are buying a new house, how much money will you need for inevitable moving-in expenses (grass seed, landscaping, new appliances, curtains, window shades, etc.)?
- Have you arranged for a low-cost homeowners insurance policy, preferably with your own insurance man?
- Do you have enough cash to buy the house and also pay for all moving-in expenses?
- Are the real estate taxes likely to go up in the area? Putting it another way, are new schools, new roads, sewers, and so on likely to be needed? Or are such services already there?

The Mortgage

● Have you talked to different mortgage lenders to determine the best mortgage terms available? In other words, have you shopped around for the best mortgage deal?

● Have you considered a VA mortgage (if you are a veteran)? An FHA mortgage?

● Does the mortgage you are getting contain a prepayment privilege? An open-end clause? A provision for including appliance and household items in the mortgage?

● Will you be able to afford the monthly payment required to pay off the mortgage? Or should you get a longer-term mortgage with smaller monthly payments?

● Have you avoided possible mortgage traps, such as a small-print clause permitting the lender to raise the interest rate later? Also, a second mortgage trap, paying "points" for a VA or FHA mortgage?

Checking the Builder

● Have you checked on the credentials and past record of the builder?

● How long has the builder been established in business locally?

● Is the name of the builder's company, the firm you are legally buying the house from, the same name and same corporation he has used in the past? If so, that's good.

● Have you talked with previous buyers of the builder's houses, asking them about their experiences with the builder?

● What kind of warranty do you get with the house?

● If it is a new house being financed with an FHA mortgage, will the house be covered by FHA's four-year protection against major defects?

● Does the builder really impress you as a well-established professional builder who will be around in the future (as he was in the past)? Or does he stir a suspicion in you that he is not as reliable as you would like?

Design of the House

- Does the house have style and genuine good looks?
- Is the house a pure architectural style, all Colonial or other traditional design? Or a true contemporary design?
- Does the house have good scale and proportion?
- Does the house have a good exposure, a good orientation in relation to the sun?
- Does the house take advantage of the best outdoor view?
- Is the house well located on its lot? Will you have privacy from the street and neighbors? Will the front area of the lot (the public zone) be easy to keep up and maintain? Will you have maximum use of your land on the sides of the house and in the back? Can you enter and leave the house quickly and conveniently?

The Floor Plan

- Does the floor plan provide good circulation in and out of the house and from one room to another?
- Are the main zones of the house—living, working, and sleeping—separated from each other?
- Do the number of floor levels—one, one-and-a-half, two stories, or split-level—offer advantages and living convenience for your family?
- Is the interior of the house bright, cheerful, and attractive?
- Does the kitchen have a central location?
- Is the kitchen well designed? Does it have an efficient work triangle, plenty of counter space and storage, a good exposure, enough space for eating?
- Is the bathroom (or bathrooms) ample and well designed and properly located for convenient access and privacy?
- Are other rooms large enough? Are they designed for attractive furniture placement?
- Are the windows large enough? Are they properly located to give ample light and a feeling of spaciousness without loss of privacy?
- Are the closets large? Is there plenty of storage for household items, linen, and laundry, as well as for clothing and personal possessions?

Buying a Used House

● Has the house been checked by a construction expert to determine if it is in structurally good condition?

● Does the price of the house compare favorably with the price of a comparable new house?

● How much money will it cost to repair, improve, and, if necessary, modernize the house? Do you have fairly accurate estimates for such work?

● How much of a total dollar investment will the house require (sales price plus total estimated cost for improvements and repairs)? Will this total investment cause the house to be over-improved for its neighborhood?

● Do you feel that the house is in good condition and is one that you really like and want?

This remodeled farmhouse in North Carolina fits naturally into its surroundings. (Photo by All About Houses)

The Construction

• Does the construction of the house conform to FHA's Minimum Property Requirements at the very least?

• Do the following important parts rate high in quality?

Foundation walls.

Termite safeguards.

Rugged, low-upkeep exterior walls and paint.

Tough interior wall surfaces.

Well-made, closely fitted flooring that will retain its appearance.

Top-quality national-brand windows and doors.

Kitchen countertop of a good plastic laminate (such as Formica), good kitchen cabinets, ample lighting and wiring outlets, and good ventilation.

Good-quality bathroom fixtures and accessories; i.e., good lavatory, tub, toilet, faucets, shower nozzle, waterproof walls and floors.

Plumbing with ¾- to 1-inch supply from the street and copper, bronze, or approved plastic piping.

Water heater with a ten-year warranty and large enough for your family.

Septic tank of 900 to 1,000 gallons' capacity and adequate leaching field, based on a percolation test that shows that the septic system will work in your ground.

Adequate electric wiring capacity: at least 240 volts and 100 amperes capacity, fifteen to twenty wiring circuits, plus spare circuits for future electric appliances.

A good roofing material of adequate weight and seal-down roof shingles.

Door hardware of solid brass, solid bronze, or solid aluminum, with a deadlock mechanism on exterior doors.

Heating, Cooling, and Insulation

• Are the walls, ceilings, and, if necessary, the floor adequately insulated? Does the insulation conform with minimum "R" value standards?

● Is the house structure lined with a vapor barrier?

● In a new house, is the heating system guaranteed to maintain the house at 70 degrees when the outdoor temperature is at its coldest level for your climate? In short, is the system large enough for the house?

● Is the heating equipment of good, if not top, quality?

● Is the heating distribution system properly designed and installed, e.g., perimeter ducts and exterior floor outlets with warm-air heat, plenty of baseboard radiation with hot-water heat, and medium- or low-density baseboards with electric heat?

● Does the heating system produce heat quickly and operate quietly? (Turn it on and see.)

● Is the fuel used, whether it's gas or oil, economical in your area? If electric heat is used, what is its estimated annual operating cost for the house?

● If the house is centrally air-conditioned, is the system capacity large enough for the house? The cooling system should be guaranteed to maintain the indoor air at no more than 75 degrees and 50 percent relative humidity when the outdoor heat is at its summer peak for your climate.

● Is the insulation adequate for air conditioning?

● Are large window areas shaded from hot sunshine to keep down heat entry, hence keep down the cooling bills?

● If it is a new house without air conditioning, are provisions made to permit easy inexpensive installation of cooling later? (Ducts and furnace blower should be large enough for cooling, a cooling-coil plenum should be installed in advance, and a spare electric circuit of adequate capacity should be installed for future air conditioning.)

Sales Gimmicks

● Does the house contain eye-catching features that may seem to have special appeal but are not necessarily of special merit? In other words, are you attracted—unknowingly, perhaps —by gimmick features?

● Do certain special features in the house tend to make you want to buy the house? Are they features that you can provide yourself in another, perhaps better, house at comparatively lower cost? Or are they intrinsic features that make it a really good house?

● What are the fundamental reasons why you and your family want a house and want the particular house you are considering?

● Have you considered seriously the kind of house you really want and need?

● Besides being of good design and construction, is the house one that you will really like and really be satisfied with? If not, and if you have *serious* doubts about it (not just the usual, natural human doubts), it's probably not the best house for you. If you do *feel* really good about it, it is probably a good, if not excellent, house for you.

Special Information on Buying and Owning a House

Become familiar with your local housing market by reading the real estate section of your local newspaper, particularly the fat weekend section. There's usually one paper in an area that dominates the real estate market and that usually publishes a special section on houses every Saturday or Sunday; in some areas it's in the Friday edition.

The monthly house ("shelter") magazines, such as *The American Home, Better Homes and Gardens, House Beautiful,* and *House & Garden,* can give you a good idea of national trends. Each is available in most public libraries and at newsstands. And each has carved out a particular sector of the house market for itself; you can choose those among them that appeal most to you.

There are also books on various aspects of buying and owning a house that can shed much light on houses. They, too, are available in most public libraries or at bookstores. Naturally we recommend the following books by the author of this book:

How to Avoid the Ten Biggest Home-Buying Traps (Hawthorn Books, $3.95).

The Homeowner's Survival Kit, all about how to reduce or eliminate the biggest home-ownership expenses, including cutting down electric bills and telephone bills, avoiding home repair bills, buying the proper house insurance, avoiding home burglary and theft, and selling a house at maximum profit (Hawthorn Books, $2.95).

The Complete Book of Home Remodeling, Improvement, and Repair, by A. M. Watkins (The Building Institute, Piermont, New York 10968. $7.50.) Please add 50¢ per book for postage and handling.

Index